Minimalism

Discover Minimalism, Declutter, And Be Stress Free Living The Lifestyle Of Simplicity In 10 Easy Steps!

I0417122

Lilly Sparks

STOP!!! Before you read any further....Would you like to know the secrets of Anti-Aging?

If your answer is yes, then you are not alone. Thousands of people are looking for the secret to reducing wrinkles, looking younger, and maintaining a youthful appearance.

If you have been searching for these answers without much luck, you are in the right place!

Not only will you gain incredible insight in this book, but because I want to make sure to give you as much value as possible, right now for a limited time you can get full **100% FREE access to a VIP bonus EBook** entitled **Anti-Aging Made Easy!**

Just Go Here For Free Instant Access:

www.LuxyLifeNaturals.com

Legal Notice

Disclaimer Notice

Table Of Contents

Introduction

I want to thank you and congratulate you for purchasing the book, *"Minimalism: Discover Minimalism, Declutter, And Be Stress Free Living The Lifestyle Of Simplicity In 10 Easy Steps!"*

This "Minimalism" book contains proven steps and strategies on how to apply the principle of minimalism in your life so that you can have a happy and meaningful life that is devoid of distractions and stress.

Minimalism entails a person to live only with the barest necessities so that he may ultimately focus on those things that he truly enjoys. For someone who is utterly consumed by material things and is drowned by a hectic lifestyle, embracing minimalism is definitely a daunting task. As such, this book is here to help you transform each day of your life from chaos into peace.

The book consists of ten chapters, which basically will answer these three fundamental questions about minimalism:

- What is minimalism?
- How can you be a minimalist?
- Can you sustain a minimalist lifestyle?

Upon unraveling the answers to these three key questions, hopefully this book can help you transform your life into a clutter-free and stress-free one by just following ten easy steps towards a minimalistic life.

Thanks again for purchasing this book, I hope you enjoy it!

Chapter 1: Reasons Behind Living A Minimalist Lifestyle

Consumerism has become entwined in everyone's lives. As you open your television for the first time during the day, after every segment of your favorite morning show you are exposed to ads about products that claim you need them, when in fact you have lived your whole life just fine without them. As you get into your car and head for work, you are still bombarded by ads – on the sidewalks, in billboards, and in posters. Advertisements are everywhere.

Ads Convert your Wants to Needs

As a consumer, for every single thing that you have, you want it to be the best. You want to achieve perfection in every way, such as having fashionable outfit, getting the trendy shoes and bags, or buying the latest gadgets. That's why advertisements lure you into buying their products through these fantasies of yours. As an example, look at these taglines and see if you aren't caught up with these brands until now.

KFC: It's finger lickin' good!

Mac Pro: Beauty outside. Beast inside.

Survivor: Outwit. Outplay. Outlast.

Disneyland: The happiest place on earth.

M&M's: Melts in your mouth, not in your hands.

Along with their catchy taglines, these brands are big spenders in marketing just to promote their products. Apple, for instance, enhances the aesthetics of their stores to entice people to come in and try their stuff. Even without a commercial, M&M's play into your imaginations through their tagline "melts in your mouth, not in your hands". All of these advertisements are created so that you will think that the product or service that a company is selling is a "need" rather than a "want".

You're Stressed on the Excesses in Your Life

Now, try to search inside of your home for any items that you may not have used for the past month. The mere idea of having items you do not use frequently is a sign that you may be accumulating things that are way past your necessity.

That's the main reason why people these days are more stressed than ever. They take in excessive things in their life. The more stuff you have, the lesser space there is in your house and more things you have to clean. In your daily lives in your home, school, or work, more work for you each day meant less time for breaks and more stress on your part.

These are the very reasons on why minimalism should become relevant for everyone. Minimalism removes these excesses in life so that one can live simply and happy.

Chapter 2: Fundamentals Of Minimalism

Whenever people say minimalist fashion, you imagine a monochromatic dress stripped off of any prints and frills. In architecture, a minimalist setting would entail a simple patch of landscape, with all the other details kept to a minimum. Similarly, a person practicing minimalism is someone who has less things to use, less things to do, but is seemingly comfortable despite all of the "lesser things in life" that he has. With these descriptions, you probably have a slightest idea on what minimalism is.

Simplicity is Beauty

In a nutshell, minimalism is being simple. You do not yearn for unnecessary things when you talk of minimalism. Case in point, if you already have enough clothes for the month, then what's the point of buying more?

Minimalism wants you to see that keeping only your favorite things, in this case your frequently-used clothes, is already enough. And in having only those things that bring you ultimate happiness, you can have more room to lavish yourself in these enjoyments that you chose.

There is beauty in less, as most minimalists say. Applying this to life, if you have fewer activities to do, it makes you less stressed. You have more time to recuperate your energy and this can translate to better health. A more happy, positive, and healthy you is indeed a sign of beauty in itself.

Shopping is a Temptation

For a minimalist, shopping is the most important activity to avoid as it tempts one to acquire and consume more. People are attracted to colorful packaging, unique designs, enchanting sounds, and fragrant scents.

Thus, even if you keep telling yourself that you are strictly window shopping, you can't be totally sure that you won't buy anything. More or less, once you have zeroed-in on one item that you like, you'll definitely go back to get it.

Clutter is Poison

A sleek and tidy house radiates of peace and calmness. The application of this principle isn't confined to your homes; you can use minimalism among your relationships too. By focusing on a small set of close friends, you can create more meaningful relationships with others. On the contrary, if you choose to be friends with everybody, you wouldn't be able to accommodate every single one of them and eventually, your relationship with those left out will suffer.

Is Minimalism Boring?

Aesthetically, people might think that having a plain home is boring. However, that's not how minimalism works. It accentuates on having less clutter on you area so that it can be more pleasing to your eyes.

Imagine a desk having a pile of unorganized papers, folders, and envelopes as compared to a desk that has none of the mess. In a minimalist desk, these papers are organized into their respective folders and envelopes and were put into a storage cabinet. The stark difference between these two desks exemplifies why minimalism is important. It keeps your life in an easier, more manageable state.

To sum it up, minimalism wants you to live within what's only necessary. Anything other than that is considered to be a clutter and should be taken away from your life.

Chapter 3: The Key Principle On How Less Is More

You may have probably been stumped by the notion that minimalism equates to having less. That is not entirely true. Instead of having less of everything, minimalism actually focuses on quality. To better explain this principle, let's examine this case.

The Minimalist Life

You wake up feeling pleased knowing that your room doesn't need that much effort to be kept tidy. Once you arrive at the office, your inbox is empty as you have already addressed all yesterday's emails. As such, once a new email has arrived, you can now focus on each of it without pressure on your part. Now the weekend arrives. You have decided to spend time with your family because they are the people that matters to you most. Overall, your life has been a breeze.

The Non-minimalist Life

If you're not a minimalist, a reverse of this situation may happen. You wake up because of a pungent smell in some part of your room. You want to find out where the source of smell is, but with all the litter around – your clothes spewed on your bed, your shoes with each pair scattered around, your books laid on every nook and cranny of your room – it's fairly impossible to find it. Since you have to go to the office in pronto, you disregard tidying your bed. It doesn't matter anyway since it's been months since you last did this chore.

Work is such a stress to you, with emails coming left and right and your boss bothering you about a report that's a week late. In fact, you can't wait for the weekend. There's a sale at the mall down the street, then after that you plan to head to your friend's house for some partying.

However, you almost forgot that your mom's birthday is in the same day as the party, so you rush towards the hotel where you all planned to celebrate her special day. You then order lavish dishes that can be bought for half the cost in another bistro on the same street. Anyway, the price doesn't matter since you have your credit card with you, but wait! You remembered that you forgot pay for your credit card dues because you have been busy for the past few weeks. With a maxed out card, now you're frantic on how you're going to pay for the meal. Finally, you exclaim, "What a hectic life this is!"

In this example, you see the disparity between a minimalist and a non-minimalist life. By focusing on the principle of "quality over quantity", the minimalist has adequate control over his life compared to the other.

Chapter 4: A Minimalist's Secret

Other people may not find minimalism to be appealing. Who wants to be left out in parties? Who doesn't want to spend a day in an expensive yacht? Who doesn't want to travel a lot, and experience a lot? Who doesn't want to buy the latest gadgets, or the lush jewelries?

Most people find happiness in this lavishness. Minimalists try to get away from these luxuries and put effort into maintaining what really makes them happy. But what is their secret in attaining a stress-free life? For a minimalist, every single thing his life falls into just two types: the Unnecessary and the Essential.

The Unnecessary and the Essential

The Unnecessary are the things that you can do away in your life. As an example, you can survive by just having the right amount of clothes. There is no need for you to purchase excess stuff, because it is highly unlikely that you may use them.

On the other hand, the Essentials are those that you think are significant to your life. Which possessions do you think are indispensable to you given your lifestyle? What events will give an impact to your family life, your social life, and your career? Minimalists place high importance on the Essentials as these are the things that keep them happy and contented.

Once you have decided on the Unnecessary and the Essential, does it stop there? Do you just blatantly label each part of your life among these two categories? Minimalism doesn't work like that. Instead, it promotes you to constantly revise these two.

As you cut down on your possessions, you gain more – more time for yourself, more freedom to do the things that you want, more opportunities to find what's really important, and ultimately, more pleasure on your part.

Minimalism is a journey of finding one's contentment in this world full of temptations. As you go towards the path of being minimalist, you will eventually learn more about yourself.

Chapter 5: How To Start Organizing Your Life

As a saying goes, "It's easier said than done." A lot of people find the minimalist's ways to be appealing, but it's much easier to think and daydream about it rather than putting these things into action.

The 360-degree Change

If you're a shop-a-holic who's so enthralled into buying clothes, shoes, and bags, putting yourself in a minimalist lifestyle is like killing the joy of your life. Just imagine, if you're shopping for at least thrice a week, can you even last a month without stepping into the mall? That's like a 360-degree change of lifestyle! It's quite similar to you starting a fitness program and not finishing the whole course. Unfortunately, not everyone has the resolve to do a full lifestyle change.

Minimalism is overwhelming, and that's even an understatement. If you wish to become a minimalist, you should be able to distract yourself from advertisements and the latest trends that you may see with others. Living with a family is much harder for a minimalist as he should be ready to face criticisms from his spouse and children. In fact, criticisms are actually the least of their problems. Having a messy person in your home would definitely bring conflicts in the near future, as you find this unruly person to ruin your minimalist lifestyle for good.

Core Values of a Minimalist

Then again, others might still want to try venturing into minimalism despite these problems. If you're one of those who are willing to embrace minimalism and all its pros and cons, here are some things you have to internalize before you embark on this lifelong journey.

1. You already have enough.

If this were a yoga class, a minimalist would repeat this mantra over and over his head. As a minimalist, you should know the importance of knowing that you're contented in life. What's the sense of throwing away needless stuff when you're just going to add it the day after?

You may argue, "I'm just starting to become a minimalist. How can I get 'quality' items if I don't buy some?" Again, contentedness is the key. Keeping track of the things you use on a daily basis is going to help you determine which of your possessions are truly worth keeping. There's no need for you to buy a better version of the item that you already have; the most important thing is you have something to use. Be contented with it.

2. Decluttering is the key step towards minimalism.

One cannot argue that the starting point in organization is through reducing the clutter. If you're striving to become a minimalist, immediately remove the unneeded things in your home, school, or office.

For someone who is fond of keeping things with sentimental value, or sees value in every little thing there is, decluttering might take a longer process to do especially if that person has an emotional connection towards an object. To address this problem, in the succeeding chapters you will learn how to declutter efficiently.

3. Time is precious.

Revisiting your possessions is just one side of a minimalist's lifestyle. Another significant aspect of your life that you need to manage is your time. Unlike objects, once time is spent you cannot bring it back anymore. That's why people always say that "Time is gold." Minimalists place enough importance on time so they always ensure that it is spent for their happiness.

With that said, you should fix your schedule in such a way that only the necessary commitments are in your planner. Also, don't forget to put enough time for rest. While time is essential, so is your body. You don't want your body to suffer by packing too many activities in a week. This is why you should only pledge to do the things that are worth your time.

4. Change is constant.

Minimalism is about finding happiness and contentment in life. One cannot control his needs and wants so minimalism allows such flexibility. It is not a rigid discipline wherein once you have deemed a possession to be unnecessary, then it will always be the case.

For instance, if your baby has outgrown his clothes, it would be fitting for you to throw or donate these things away. But what if suddenly you are expecting another child in the family? The infant clothes will now be considered essential in this case.

By keeping these values in mind, you should be able to discern whether minimalism is for you or not. These four core values govern a minimalist's mindset, and if you do not agree with these ideals then it's time for you to bid adieu of your dreams of having a minimalist lifestyle.

Chapter 6: 10 Easy Steps To Declutter Your Life

Cleaning is an easy chore; you simply wipe out the dirt and grime in your belongings then you're done. Decluttering is another matter. Besides cleaning your mess, you assess all the items that you have and expunge everything that's unneeded. That's a tough job to do especially if you're not aware of which things are really useless. As such, below are the guidelines on how you can proceed to decluttering.

1. Decide on which area you should start.

You can't possibly proceed in decluttering places all at the same time. More often than not, that's a sure way of how you can easily misplace things. So instead of being able to focus, it will just cause you to work harder. It's understandable that you're excited about decluttering, but getting ahead in the process without much thinking will get you nowhere. To start, in which areas should you start decluttering? Where are you usually working? Determine the places which you usually frequent to; that should be your starting place.

2. Remove everything in the area.

It'll be much easier if you work on a clean slate rather than work in parts. For instance, if you're going to declutter your cabinet in this way, it would be hard for you to reorganize things since it's already full.

3. Make a quick decision on the item: Do you really need it or not?

When you say declutter, you're not going to take all items out then put them back in, albeit in an organized way. That's like putting all your belongingsin the same place as the garbage. So before you put your stuff in its rightful place, decide if you still need it or not. Here are a couple of questions to help you in your choice: Is it a valuable item (e.g., jewelry)? Can you survive without it?

4. For those items with a sentimental value, take a picture.

Usually, it's these types of items that end up in your storage unmoved for a long time. That's why minimalists don't hold into physical things and they'd much rather cherish these items in a more practical way. Scrapbooks usually end up in the attic, and people wouldn't have noticed it at all if they didn't clean the area. Now that you've found your own scrapbook in the attic (thanks to this book!), is it even economical to store it again for a couple of years more? Here's a great alternative: take a picture of it. Once you store it digitally, you can now easily retrieve it for your personal use. Or better, you can share it with your friends in popular social networks such as Facebook.

5. Throw any item that you haven't used within the past six months.

After doing steps 1 and 4, you still find yourself with a considerable amount of possessions that you think can still be whittled down. Here's another tip: if you haven't used an item within six months, throw it out. Chances are you probably wouldn't need it in the succeeding months ahead. For seasonal items such as winter clothes, you can probably extend the time to one years, i.e., have you used it for the past year?

6. If you're not sure about whether to throw an item or not, you can put them in the "Undecided" box.

Don't ever make the mistake of putting an "undecided" item along with your essential items; it will probably just rot in the storage. Just put them in the "undecided" box, but make sure that you've already decided within weeks' time on these items. If it'll take you longer, that box might as well be another clutter in your room and you don't want that to happen.

7. Before you put everything back, clean the surface first.

Besides having a tidier area, you don't want to trigger certain allergies because of unsanitary practices.

8. Don't simply put each item back, create a separate area for each.

You're done with segregating the unnecessary items from the essentials, as well as cleaning the place up. However, if you're going to put these items back in whatever way you like, it will look like you just had the clutter back. As such, be sure to separate each item and put them in their respective places. For instance, your clothes should be lined up according to kind. T-shirts and pants should be neatly folded, and is separately stored from your underwear. Once you're done, you'll see how neat and organized your decluttered area is.

9. Repeat these steps again in another area.

Decluttering doesn't stop there. Repeat these steps in the other areas in the house. Only then can you proceed to declutter outside your home.

10. Either donate or throw your Unnecessary items.

As a saying goes, "One man's trash is another man's treasure." Before you throw out all your unnecessary things, look for items which you can donate such as clothes and toys.

With these ten easy steps, decluttering will never be a daunting task any more. In the next chapter, you will also learn how to "declutter" other areas of your life.

Chapter 7: 10 Practical Steps In Simplifying Your Life

Now to the nitty-gritty part of the book, here are the ten practical steps on how you can simplify your life – the minimalist way. Wait, is that even possible? How can you be a minimalist by just doing 10 steps?

Unfortunately, there is no shortcut towards being a minimalist. If that were the case, a lot would have become minimalist by now. Most people are unconsciously tied up to the habit of achieving more, thus making it impossible for one to turn into a full-fledged minimalist overnight.

Instead of "steps", you should rather take the following items below as "phases". Each phase corresponds to every possible facet of your life – your family/home, your finances, your health, and so on. For every item, you will be reading recommendations on how you can further simplify each area.

1. Turn your home into a minimalist haven.

Your home is your refuge. This is where you seek for inspiration and energy for you to last the whole day. However, if your home is too unkempt for decent use, it may not serve its purpose well. As such, the minimalist ensures that their home is neat and organized.

With the number of rooms in your house, where should you start? It is recommended that you start in your room. This is so that whenever you step into your personal space, it may serve as your inspiration to continue your journey towards minimalism. Afterwards, you can proceed to the common areas such as living room, dining room, kitchen and bathroom.

 It is indeed boring if the living room that once housed all your pictures, figurines, and furnishings were now removed. While minimalism wants you to remove the non-essentials, it also recognizes that aesthetics is indispensable. Thus, for a minimalist setup, look for a simple yet elegant centerpiece that will be the focal point of room. The walls and floors then should be painted in a solid yet muted shade.

2. Purge your closet.

You also apply the same rule as above, keep the essentials and store the rest. But what if you have so many clothes that you cannot discern which one is essential? You can use an outfit formula. This considers the activities that you do on a daily basis.

Let's say that you're a legal assistant at a major law firm. You wear corporate attire for five days a week. On weekends, you usually go to the mall to unwind, and you only don a casual getup. In this scenario, you have two outfit formulas: the Blazer + blouse + skirt/pants and Blouse + short/pants. Now considering these minimalist numbers of clothing:

Work: 2 Blazer + 4 blouse + 3 skirt/2 pants (11 items) = 40 outfits

Casual: 4 Blouse + 3 short/3 pants (10 items) = 24 outfits

If you do the math, you can wear 64 outfit combinations in using these garments. And if you mix your work and casual pieces together, you can make at least 176 outfits. That's like almost half a year worth of clothing! No one would even notice that you're wearing the same thing.

3. Create a minimalistic workstation.

Are you familiar with the process improvement tool called 5S? Among its teachings is that in your office, you should only have five items on your work desk. For instance, you can keep the following items in your table: mug, planner, a picture frame, a pen, and a pen holder. These items should be enough for you to do your work efficiently. All the other items beyond the limit should be kept in the storage area.

4. Go paperless.

You can do away with the sticky notes and the hard copies of reports, as you can just message your co-worker through a personal messenger, or secure an electronic copy of the report through email.

While it's good for you to go paperless, gadgets such as cellphones and tablets are a big distraction to your work. To be more efficient in your workplace, better keep them away.

5. Eat healthy.

Eating is a pleasurable activity. However, most people consider it to be their pastime instead of just an activity to nourish their body. In turn, they only harm their health in the long run by eating too much.

A minimalist only eats less, but he ensures that he is well-nourished. This is done through "clean eating". If you eat food in its natural state, you preserve the vitamins and minerals that it contains. Thus, your body is able to digest and absorb your food without the preservatives and the cholesterol brought about by cooking. Practicing vegetarianism is for extreme minimalists, and is not for everyone.

6. Have time to exercise.

You don't have to hit the gym in order to keep yourself fit. Besides paying for expensive fees, going to the gym will take away much time due to travel. Therefore, you should find ways on how you can exercise each day without resorting to the gym.

An example would be to go jogging for about half an hour. If your school or office is just blocks away from your residence, you can just jog your way towards home. To make your exercise more challenging, you can use fitness equipment such as dumbbell, jump rope, or a chin up bar for an overall body workout.

7. Manage your finances well.

As you trim your needs and wants to a minimum, you now realize its huge impact to your finances. But if it's not enough, you can do these three things to manage your money well:

1) *Don't go into debt.* Having debt only induces stress on your part. Therefore, you should refrain from using credit cards and just use cash or debit card instead.

2) *Save up.* Your excess cash should not be spent further. It should be kept up in the bank or put under an investment for better use.

3) *Use the auto-pay feature.* There's a facility in banks wherein you can automatically pay for your bills through your payroll, so that when you receive your net pay you will never have to worry about the bills.

8. Keep your grooming products to a minimum.

Men are generally simple when it comes to grooming products. All they need is a shampoo and soap, a deodorant, and a shaver – and that's it. They're already covered from head to toe.

On the other hand, women are much meticulous when it comes to their grooming needs. For their face, they use a plethora of creams and powders such as moisturizer, foundation, blush-on, mascara, eyeliner, lipstick, and so on. With the number of products mentioned, that does not even include their grooming items for their hair, body, feet, and nails, and other beauty products that they use at night.

It's no wonder that women take a lot of time in preparing themselves for a day. A minimalist woman, however, focuses on taking good care of her body instead of concealing her appearance through makeup. As such, she can do away in using all these beauty products.

9. Travel light.

Going to the beach is a perfect getaway to relax and unwind. However, you might not really achieve the "relax and unwind" especially if you're bringing your whole closet with you. Isn't it stressful if you were to carry such weight in your vacation? Only bring the essential things with you, such as toiletries and clothes. You don't have to bring your laptop with you, or your whole shoe rack.

Also, travelling light isn't confined to your belongings, but it includes your itinerary. It's understandable that you want to visit many landmarks and do many outdoor activities while you're on vacation. However, if you cram too much tasks in one day, wouldn't that make you more stressed? A vacation should be a day where you don't have to put on much importance on deadlines; your school or office work already does that for you. Therefore, make sure that you have a lot of leeway in your itinerary so that you can leisurely enjoy your planned vacation.

10. Unclutter your computer desktop.

Most people usually prefer to save their files in their desktop for easy access. However, it might be too late when they realize that having a bunch of random icons in your desktop will only make the searching longer. As such, it is better if you save your files in their respective folders in the Documents area. As for the programs, you can just pin its icon in the taskbar so that you don't have to put a shortcut in your desktop.

As you've noticed, there is no timeline given for each phases. What will you do first? How long will each phase take? Because people don't have the same priorities and circumstances, there is no cookie-cutter timetable that can be applied to everyone. The best thing you can do is to create your own schedule for each phase, considering how much of a minimalist you want to be.

Chapter 8: Blocking Out Distractions And Stress

Distractions and stress are the main hindrance in your journey towards minimalism. External forces such as your family and friends may influence you along the way, thereby affecting your minimalist ways. To help you counteract these problems, here are some tips.

1. Plan your schedule with adjustments in mind.

Most of the time, your day doesn't go to how you planned it. That's why it's important if you put on some leeway in your schedule. Don't attempt to cram up every meeting or deadline within the day; it will surely bring you stress. Also, this may result to you not being able to focus on the task at hand, which can further affect all your pending activities or jobs.

2. Learn how to say no.

Usually, your schedule are always full not because you have so many plans for yourself but rather because you agree to other people's events. If you want to free up your schedule, learn to say no especially to those activities that you think are not important. Be sure to spend time with people that really matter and avoid creating a network of estranged friends.

3. Take a break.

People usually forget to allot time for themselves. They wanted to keep abreast of the latest buzz so they spend their time in every event that they could join, not knowing that it's their body that's taking a toll on all these activities. As a minimalist, take time to relax. Make sure that you've rejuvenated at least a day per week so that you can face the next week relieved from stress.

Since the distractions and stress are out of the way, you're now ready to learn the steps on how to sustain the minimalist habits. In the succeeding chapters, you will be informed of the ways on how to maintain such lifestyle and the mistakes that you should avoid along the way.

Chapter 9: Mistakes To Avoid

Minimalism is a habit of decluttering. You do a constant edit of your life so that you can achieve a more efficient you. However, there are times when people tend to go back to their old selves. What are the reasons behind this?

1. Going to sales.

In every payday and every holiday, stores give discountson their products and services. Usually, there are three gimmicks that stores do so that you can buy more: a 50 to 70% discount on an item, a Buy 2 Take 1 scheme, and buying on bulk for big discounts. Although you may get these stuff for a fewer bucks, you will end up having more items than you need. As such, minimalists don't approach sales as an advantageous event.

2. Getting lured by points and freebies.

Credit cards entice you to spend more by giving you points for every purchase. Also, some merchants give freebies in exchange of buying a certain amount in their stores. Don't be fooled by their strategies. Stick to your needs and don't buy in excess.

3. Believing the advertisements.

Ads are created with customers in mind. Whatever excites your senses, marketers tap on to that so that you'll buy their products. Why shouldn't you believe in advertisements? Remember that you have lived your entire life just fine even without using these products that they are advertising.

4. Spending time in social media sites.

Are you envious of the brand new car that your boss has posted in Facebook? Do you want to get a hold of the new pair of sneakers that you saw on Instagram? These social media sites are so prevalent today that companies use it as an avenue to advertise their products and services. If you stay away from these sites, you're doing yourself a favor.

5. Buying in impulse.

Have you spotted an item that you wanted to get at that very moment? Well, if you bought it, that's called an impulse, buy. As a minimalist, you can't have yourself buying all sorts of things in a whim. You have to think before you buy. If after 30 days you figured that you need the item, then only then can you buy it.

Even with the numerous sources in books, magazines, and the internet about minimalism, how come people still find it hard to turn their life into a minimalist one? A famous line sums it up: "Old habits die hard." It is now up to you to fight all these vices in life that you've grown accustomed to. Make the core values of minimalism as your mantra every day. Eventually, you'll be able to resist these temptations on your own using just pure mindset.

Chapter 10: Maintaining Minimalism

Through this book, you have learned the different steps on how to embrace minimalism. However, minimalism is not just a one-step process. Instead, it's a continuous learning for you every day, as you declutter your life and finding out what matters to you most.

Enjoy the Simple Life

People usually try doing some of the steps for a week, and then find themselves going back in their sorry, cluttered state the week after. Why is the reversal too soon? Most probably, these people don't appreciate what the simple life has to offer them. However, you really won't be able to see the positive effects of minimalism if you're going to spend only a week in it. So before you give up, take time to study and learn the principles behind minimalism.

As you transition towards a minimalist life, look for the changes happening in yourself as well as the changes on the people around you. Do you think you are better now than you were before? What are the comments of people regarding your new habits? Has minimalism become a positive influence in your life?

Respect Other People's Beliefs

Not everyone will understand on why you're living with the barest necessities. "Why skip on life's luxuries when you only have one life to live?", most people would say. Minimalists find pleasure in living a simple and stress-free life. Other people don't think that way and you should respect that.

Whenever you're dealing with your family, be very patient about it. Teach them on the ways on how to live a simple life, without you even telling them about the virtues of minimalism. As you all change your lives for the better, they will eventually understand and appreciate minimalism.

If ever you feel like giving up, read this book again and be reminded of the reasons on why you started your journey towards minimalism. Hopefully, you should be able to find peace and contentedness once you're done with all the steps mentioned.

In fact, picking up this book is just one step of the process. So you better congratulate yourself by finishing the first but crucial step, which is learning the fundamentals of minimalism.

Conclusion

Thank you again for purchasing the book *"Minimalism: Discover Minimalism, Declutter, And Be Stress Free Living The Lifestyle Of Simplicity In 10 Easy Steps!"*

I am extremely excited to pass this information along to you, and I am so happy that you now have read and can hopefully implement these strategies going forward.

I hope this book was able to help you understand the fundamentals of minimalism and how to you can apply this principle in every facet of your life – in your home, in your school or office, and even in your relationships.

The next step is to get started using this information and to hopefully live a stress-free and clutter-free life through minimalism!

Please don't be someone who just reads this information and doesn't apply it, the strategies in this book will only benefit you if you use them!

If you know of anyone else that could benefit from the information presented here please inform them of this book.

Finally, if you enjoyed this book and feel it has added value to your life in any way, please take the time to share your thoughts and post a review on Amazon. It'd be greatly appreciated!

Thank you and good luck!

Preview Of:

Simple Meditation For Beginners!

Meditation

Learn Mindfulness Meditation Techniques And Basics Of How To Meditate, Simplify Your Life, Gain Spirituality, Quiet Your Mind, And Increase Positivity!

.

Introduction

I want to thank you and congratulate you for purchasing the book, *"Meditation: Simple Meditation For Beginners! Learn Mindfulness Meditation Techniques and Basics of How to Meditate, Simplify Your Life, Gain Spirituality, Quiet Your Mind, and Increase Positivity!"*

This book contains proven steps and strategies on how to practice meditation in order to live in the present moment and be more fulfilled in life. This book will help you reap the benefits of meditation, live a simpler, but happier life, and acquire a positive outlook in life. This book will help you understand the benefits of meditation and how you can use it to improve the quality of your life.

If you feel that you are just living day after day without a sense of purpose, if you feel that your life has no sense of direction. If you feel stressed, ill, and tired of all the pressures and demands of life, this is for you.

This book will help you learn the ancient techniques of meditation that will help you quiet your mind and discover the most important things in life. This book will help you live a better, brighter, and more positive life.

Thanks again for purchasing this book, I hope you enjoy it!

Chapter 1: Why Must You Start Meditating NOW!?

Meditation is very popular nowadays. In fact, it has become a buzz word in the "new age" community. Many people are jumping into the meditation and yoga bandwagon because these practices have been frequently featured in many magazines, websites, and popular talk shows such as Oprah. Many celebrities like Jennifer Aniston, Paula Abdul, Kristen Bell, Sheryl Crow, Jim Carrey, Ellen DeGeneres, Mia Farrow, Jane Fonda, Hugh Jackman, Nicole Kidman, Naomi Watts, Miranda Kerr, and Madonna practice meditation regularly.

Meditation is popular because of its ability to relax and calm the mind. In this age when everyone is all busy and tired, we need something that will help us become grounded. We need something that will protect us from all the stress, anxiety, and pressures.

Here are the most compelling reasons why you should start meditating now:

1. Improved Concentration – Stress, pressures, and aging often cause your mind to deteriorate. Because of these factors, you will often have problems with cognition and other brain functions which would make it difficult for you to concentrate and focus. Meditation is a mental practice or a form of mental training that will enhance your concentration and focus. If you meditate regularly, it will be easier for you to do study, write, or concentrate on a very important task. When you meditate regularly, you will not be easily distracted by the internet or social networking sites.

2. Improved Function of the Immune System – Because meditation is a relaxation technique, it helps strengthen the immune system. Meditation improves the body's resistance to various diseases and it helps the body fight cancer cells and viruses. If you noticed that your health has been deteriorating and that you are now more prone to flu and fever, then it is high time to start meditating before it's too late.

3. Increased Fertility – Studies show that women who meditate often are more fertile than those who do not. A study also shows that men who meditate often have increased sperm count.

4. Meditation Lowers the Blood Pressure – A study conducted at the Harvard Medical School show that regular meditation practitioners have lower blood pressure. When your blood pressure is lower, your body is less likely to react to stress hormones.

5. Meditation eases stress and anxiety – Meditation is known to reduce stress and anxiety. If you are constantly exposed to stressful tasks, relationships, and circumstances, then it is best to meditate regularly.

6. Calmness – Meditation calms the nerves and it helps the practitioners to be more relaxed. Meditation helps you keep your cool even when faced with stressful situations and circumstances.

7. Emotional stability – Meditation helps practitioners become more grounded and in control of their emotions. Emotions are sometimes erratic. Emotions can entrap you and make you feel as if you are on a roller coaster where you experience frequent twists and turns, ups and down. Meditation can help you clear your mind of all the negativity. It can help you deal with emotional baggage. It can also help you gain clarity and peace of mind.

8. Increased creativity – Some forms of meditation, like the ones that aim to awaken the Kundalini energy, can increase creativity. People who practice advanced meditation techniques often experience a spontaneous flow of creative ideas. Regular meditation practitioners become more imaginative and artistic. Steve Jobs, who was a meditation practitioner, credits his spiritual practice for his renewed creativity when he founded Pixar.

9. Meditation lessens susceptibility to critics – People who meditate regularly are less vulnerable to critics and detractors. They are less likely to take things too

personally. Meditation also enables practitioners to quiet their inner critic and accept themselves more.

10. Meditation helps your true north – If you are already in your early thirties or forties, but you still have not figured out what to do then it is time to meditate. Meditation helps you get in touch with your true purpose. Meditation helps you become more in touch with what you really want out of life.

11. Meditation improves intuition – Meditation brings you clarity and this strengthens your intuition, your inner guide. Meditation helps you understand yourself better. Meditation brings your soul and spirit in tune with the divine and that of other people. You will have some flashes of insight and higher knowledge. It would be easier for you to make the right decisions and determine the true nature of people, despite of the masks that they wear.

12. Meditation brings you closer to the divine – Prayer is actually a form of meditation. Meditation is known to bring you closer to the Divine power. It helps you connect with the Higher Energy and brings you closer to God.

13. Meditation cultivates compassion – Meditation helps you become more connected and empathetic towards others. As a result, you will become more compassionate and understanding towards others. This will in turn help you build stronger and deeper relationships with people around you.

If you have been stressed, tired, sick, and you feel that your life is getting nowhere, it is recommended to start meditating now. Meditation has a lot of health, emotional, and mental benefits that will help your life become better, happier, and more fulfilling.

Thanks For Previewing My Exciting Book Entitled:

"Meditation: Simple Meditation For Beginners! Learn Mindfulness Meditation Techniques And Basics Of How To Meditate, Simplify Your Life, Gain Spirituality, Quiet Your Mind, And Increase Positivity!"

To purchase this book, simply go to the Amazon Kindle store and simply search:

"MEDITATION"

Then just scroll down until you see my book. You will know it is mine because you will see my name "Lilly Sparks" underneath the title.

Alternatively, you can visit my author page on Amazon to see this book and other work I have done. Thanks so much, and please don't forget your free bonuses

DON'T LEAVE YET! - CHECK OUT YOUR FREE BONUSES BELOW!

Free Bonus Offer: Get Free Access To The www.LuxyLifeNaturals.com VIP Newsletter!

Once you enter your email address you will immediately get free access to this awesome newsletter!

But wait, right now if you join now for free you will also get free access to the "Anti-Aging Made Easy" free EBook!

To claim both your FREE VIP NEWSLETTER MEMBERSHIP and your FREE BONUS Ebook on ANTI-AGING MADE EASY!

Just Go To:

www.LuxyLifeNaturals.com

www.ingramcontent.com/pod-product-compliance
Lightning Source LLC
Chambersburg PA
CBHW070934290526
45795CB00003B/1015